1st Recital Series

FOR F HORN

Including works of:
- James Curnow
- Craig Alan
- Douglas Court
- Mike Hannickel
- Timothy Johnson
- Ann Lindsay

Solos for Beginning
through Early Intermediate
level musicians

CURNOW® MUSIC

EXCLUSIVELY DISTRIBUTED BY

HAL•LEONARD® CORPORATION

7777 W. BLUEMOUND RD. P.O. BOX 13819 MILWAUKEE, WI 53213

Edition Number: CMP 0761-02-400

1st Recital Series
Solos for Beginning through Early Intermediate level musicians
Horn

ISBN: 978-90-431-1748-7

CD Accompaniment tracks performed by Becky Shaw

CD number: 19.030-3 CMP

Foreword

High quality solo/recital literature that is appropriate for performers playing at the Beginner through Early Intermediate skill levels is finally here! Each of the **1st RECITAL SERIES** books is loaded with exciting and varied solo pieces that have been masterfully composed or arranged for your instrument.

Included with the solo book is a professionally recorded CD that demonstrates each piece. Use these examples to help develop proper performance practices. There is also a recording of the accompaniment alone that can be used for performance (and rehearsal) when a live accompanist is not available. A separate Piano Accompaniment book is available [edition nr. CMP 0762.02].

Table of Contents

Solo with accompaniment

Accompaniment

1. SHADOWS OF THE PAST

Mike Hannickel
(ASCAP)

5

Track 4 5 F HORN

2. ANCIENT TOWERS

Craig Alan (ASCAP)

3. ANTHEM

Mike Hannickel (ASCAP)

4. EVENING SHADOWS Timothy Johnson (ASCAP)

Copyright © 2002 by **Curnow Music Press, Inc.**

Franz Schubert
5. SANCTUS

Arr. **James Curnow** (ASCAP)

6. TRUMPET VOLUNTARY

Jeremiah Clarke
Arr. **Ann Lindsay** (ASCAP)

10

7. COPPER AND ZINC

Ann Lindsay (ASCAP)

8. MARCH MAJESTIC

Douglas Court (ASCAP)

Allegro e maestoso (♩ = 132)

9. THE BRITISH GRENADIERS

Traditional
Arr. **James Curnow** (ASCAP)

10. THE RED BALLOON

James Curnow (ASCAP)

Copyright © 2002 by Curnow Music Press, Inc.

11. EXCURSION

Timothy Johnson (ASCAP)

W. A. Mozart
12. ANDANTE
from LA CI DAREM LA MANO
From Don Giovanni

Arr. **Ann Lindsay** (ASCAP)